THE POET'S
GARAGE

TERRY TIERNEY

Attention schools and businesses: for discounted copies on large orders, please contact the publisher directly. Books are brought to the trade by Ingram.

For information contact:

Unsolicited Press

Portland, Oregon

www.unsolicitedpress.com

orders@unsolicitedpress.com

619-354-8005

Photo Credit: Ben Krantz

Cover Design: Kathryn Gerhardt

Editor: Saidah Wilson

ISBN: 978-1-950730-41-4

Library of Congress: 2019954604

For Michaelyn

TABLE OF CONTENTS

Renovations   9

    Painting the House White   10

    How to Build a House   12

    Blue Jay   13

    Her White Tattoo   15

    What the Seagulls Know   17

    House Slide   18

    The Lives of a Cell   19

    Weeping Willows Green First   21

    My Old Furnace   22

    Widow's Peak   24

    The Poet's Garage   25

    My Third Divorce   27

Shadows and Dreams   31

    The Man Who Never Dreams   32

    Her Collection of Knives   34

    Wine Stains   36

    Her Names   38

    The Empty Bottle   40

The Poisoned Blood · 42

Light and Shadow · 44

Last Words · 46

Two Women Leaving the Church · 47

Poem with Nude · 48

At the Leonard Cohen Concert · 49

Comfort Food · 51

Water's Edge · 53

Weather Report · 54

Life Line · 56

Snow Squall · 58

Cider Press · 60

Ice Age · 61

The Museum of Personal History · 62

Reading the Signs · 63

The Empress of Iowa Sheds Her Disguise · 64

Turning Back at the Rubicon · 66

The Rattlesnake Exchanges Its Skin · 67

Smelling the Rain · 68

Door of Echoes · 71

The Boxer's Choice · 72

Grandfather Fishing · 74

My Only Home Run   75

Shaky Charlie Talks About His Youth   76

What to Do in Case of a Gas Attack   78

My Father's Tools   79

Learning How to Dream   81

When It Was Dark Enough   83

Family Dinner   85

Bluegill   87

The Crossing   89

Renovations

PAINTING THE HOUSE WHITE

Paint thick in the August heat
never seems to dry, moist air
heavy with sweat and mosquitoes,
resists my running strokes. Grey oak and cedar,
parched from years of neglect, thirst
for white paint—old browns and bare trim
glow whiter with each dip and slap.
I whiten also. Splashes stick
to my skin like scabs,
hot pores open, unprimed wood.

I remember that summer we painted
the house brown, how my rough
hands seemed to melt her skin,
chocolate tan, and how the flecks
of white light on the river below us
disappeared as we marked them
like details of a dream. Looking
down from my ladder, I watched
her long strides cross State Street bridge.
We never spoke after she left.
She seemed to shrink with time

like green lumber, her limbs a silhouette
of fallen branches on that autumn day
when I thought I saw her kneeling
on the river bank to sketch a dead perch
washed up on the dark, wet slate.

In the evenings I saw her often,
a brown shadow leaning against my porch post,
her face to the lights of the valley,
her flesh blood warm—present even now
in every strip of wood I paint.

Tonight I watch mosquitoes rush
the sticky white, as if it were bare skin,
and flail their dark wings in whiteness,
the white of death and forgetting.
The hot enamel dries slow as blood.

HOW TO BUILD A HOUSE

First, wait until the snow clears.
Pull on rubber boots with wide soles,
so you will not damage the carpet.

Walk until you find a depression
where deer have rested in tall grass.
Here you will sleep.

Walk out of the bedroom and turn in a circle
until your eyes water, facing the wind.
Here you will place your chair.

The roof is self-explanatory,
but walls are something you will raise yourself.
Be sure to plan your windows.

Now call your friends
and gather sticks for a fire.

If it snows before daybreak,
you will have to begin again.

Blue Jay

Lances down from red maple,
squirrel darting in retreat,
clutching phone line, ducking for cover.

I sense the airborne threat,
trying to pick cherries, a boy
with courage only for ground fall,

the blue jay's screech and swoop
protecting even rotten fruit.
I fill the bird bath to distract him,

his sharp beak and talons
claim cherries and water, staining
the basin red with skins and pits.

My family moves to a new town,
then another, each house white,
a three-bedroom ranch where blue jay

perches in the backyard tree:
redwood, box elder, catalpa, spruce.
Blue jay always the same.

It was years before he found me here,
my own ranch house,
my cherry seedling.

When he lights on my window sill,
I know what he will say.
Every move disturbs his nest.

There's only one house, one tree,
one blue jay the color of sky.

HER WHITE TATTOO

I remember how it began,
how the houses he painted
seemed to frame her poems,
how her words grew there, filling rooms
as she read them, pressing on windows
and doors like fumes of a dream
trying to breathe into waking.

In the rooms where he worked,
she smelled the fresh odor of paint,
linseed oil and mineral spirits, each pigment
a different scent, and she traced
his strokes along the trim of every room:
above, below, all edges sanded.

In her mind she painted rooms
he never touched, knowing
the twist of his hands, the dip
and spread of his fingers, a dancer's
stroke dissolving darkness.

Even in a room she just rented
miles away, she recalls his touch
and the print of her bare shoulder
on the wet frame of the dining room door
that morning she leaned there, reciting
a midnight poem. Some lines
she never forgets. They adhere
to her skin like a bandage.

What the Seagulls Know

The pencil breaks in your hand,
lines too taut to hold,
ocean still as a desert,
only water, no gulls.

Most of them have flown here.
They pace the room expectantly,
staring as I write.
I know why they came.

I nest them in manuscripts.
Gulls defend the balconies,
gulls eat pastry in Central Park,
shrieking gulls invade my sleep.

I mail them back to you.
Artist, lover, keeper,
I dip my wings to your shore.

HOUSE SLIDE

The storm blows first in my mind,
wind and water spinning, shade trees
leaning down the grade, pushed by channels
of mud and stone,
pressing piers of our foundation.

Rain strikes the roof and pounds
us deeper, streaming over gutters
stuffed with leaves, down the shingles
I should have painted,
seeping through cracks in the driveway,
through chipped grout between bricks,
pooling on basement tiles.

We begin to slide,
the earth flowing underground
like the shadow of our summers,
shaded memories of eucalyptus trees
cracking now with water weight,
roots ripping free.

THE LIVES OF A CELL

I can't remember being one cell,
my sensations in that first moment
before I began to divide. But years later

I recalled the odor of lilacs,
holding a wilted sprig in my hand,
the water in the wine bottle tepid
like a stagnant bacterial pond.

Lilac fragrance filled our rooms for days,
impossible to escape, subsuming us
when we toasted the first warm sun
with cheap rose and saved the empty bottles.

Now I remember nothing but lilacs,
how they stayed after you left,
so there was never any need for letters,
the stale water digesting the fallen petals

until I had to dump the bottles
to erase the sour smell, unable to recover
the fragrance or the brightest sun
before maples exploded with leaves.

I see you are building a new house
room by room, southern exposure, a bed
for lilacs. It looks odd to me,
rising so abruptly among startled pines,
but I have no eye for architecture.

Weeping Willows Green First

Years ago when we brought them here,
their roots tied in rice sacks,
we thought none would survive.

We treated them like refugees,
helped the adults adjust to the climate,
let the young look out for themselves.

Now they sprout like green flares,
thriving in our neglect,
among the hillsides of dormant trees.

My Old Furnace

The squat torso and thick bandaged arms
held up my house. I remember
the click and small explosion,
the cracking of wooden vents
as my house swelled with warmth.
My pipes never froze.

My friends argued for efficiency.
Built for coal and wood, converted to oil,
the furnace filled one-third of my cellar.

I did the work myself,
tearing loose the grasp of old vents,
finding lost passages and compartments
with papers too stained and brittle to read,
picking the floor joists bare as bones.

The furnace resisted,
sheet metal shroud repelling my hammer
until one by one, rivets popped free,
revealing the cast iron core,

welded baffles thick with rust,
too wide for my cellar door and windows.
My house was built for the furnace.

Installing the gas model was easy,
light enough to slide into place,
narrow vents crimping together
with pliers. I needed help
to shove the old core off its concrete slab
where it remains on the dirt floor,
a collapsed ruin,
the new furnace rising up beside it
like a condominium.

Each summer I say I'll hire a welder
to cut it in pieces and haul it off.
My resolve fades as I brace for winter,
arms heavy, cellar cold,
waiting for the warmth to come.

WIDOW'S PEAK

You string a necklace of washed up shells,
lance them with pins to drain the sea,
and wish they had always been silent.

They remind you of the wind in the orchard
where apples fell like footsteps,
the sound receding still.

Like decaying fruit, they leave their skins.
Their cores shrivel to nothing but sound,
the persistent echo of ocean.

Waves crash on the rocks below,
piercing the silence of your empty room,
and call you as they called others

to discard your shell or take it with you.
But you're not prepared to leave,
and your room is too much to carry.

The Poet's Garage

When the policemen come to arrest me
for forgery, I hide out in the garage
where I learned how to write, my manual
laid out on the bench, words stacked around me
like old tires, pools of black grease
where lines have spilled, staining the sawdust.

I watch the detective study the house,
his junkie nose running, he anticipates
my arrest and waits for my wife to come home
from the library. He reads her the charge,
how I forged checks in three counties.
The name is right but the description fails,

the forger stands taller, pounds heavier,
a different smith. *My husband looks like a mechanic,*
she says, *and he's much older.* I grin
my toothless grin, holding a bucket of greasy words.
A blue-suited sergeant refuses
to believe her, saying I am both

smaller and larger, older and younger,
a mechanic and a smith. Look in the garage,
she says. Modifiers hanging on nails,
the cardboard box of active verbs, files
of proper nouns. No signatures remain,
the author gone, only spaces where he worked.

They gather the spaces for evidence.
I escape with the narrative, some of it
leaking on the way, until my book breaks down
in Pennsylvania. When my wife escapes
and brings my tools, I begin to forge
a new silence, a new name, a new library.

My Third Divorce

My first divorce is a hippie divorce. We have few worldly possessions other than our record collection and our philosophy. We remember who bought each of the records, but the philosophy has no origin we can identify. We don't fight over the wire spool, our major piece of furniture, or our Sears portable stereo. Since we never got around to having children, there is no custody fight, except for the dog, a black and white beagle mix my wife rescued from the pound. When he brings home the blackened carcasses of chickens and other animals, she says they are gifts for me. She claims he loves me best. You take him, she says. No, you take him. We agree on a visitation schedule carefully planned with intervals for cleaning and disinfectants. I consider running away when it is my turn, but he runs away before I can. I know he survives to terrorize another neighborhood and sire a pack of vicious little dogs. One day, I expect the pack to come for me.

My first divorce is the beginning of my second divorce, a cycle of nature. We have another dog, a huge black dog with a pack of his own, my second wife and me. Early in our marriage, we buy an old farmhouse with tall windows and no curtains because the sunlight is good for plants. In the winter, the wind blows through loose wallboards and snow collects on the inside corners of windowsills. Deep in the cellar, an oil furnace with thick octopus arms pushes heat up through floor vents and out the cracks. The furnace holds up the house and lifts plants closer to the sun.

My wife raises the plants. We argue about the house as it leans uncertainly on its stone foundation over the dirt basement. We argue about mud and floods in the basement whenever it rains and we fight about the holes in the roof. You take the house, she says. No, you take it. In the end, the big dog takes the house, his bright yellow eyes requiring me to stay. We trade the expensive stereo for the bank account, the car for the payments. She leaves the plants, as a thief leaves her conscience behind to go on a raid. The scratching behind the walls and window frames start about the time she leaves.

At night when I try to find the source of the scratching, the plants close around me, their leaves thrashing in forced air. Bright and green during daylight, the rooms collapse into a primordial forest, forbidden and lethal. Even though I water and feed the plants as loyally as a monk, they follow me like prey. I consider withholding their water and letting them die, but I am certain they read my thoughts.

The dog tracks me around the house when I can't sleep for the racket, but the plants never threaten him. He is part of the jungle. I take comfort in his presence, in case the pack of demon dogs breaks through the rotten timbers, bent on revenge, or if the plants make a pre-emptive strike. Maybe my ex-wife scratches on the windows and walls, hoping to prove her arguments about my elusive sanity. The big dog would never bark at her. I keep him well fed.

He chooses my third wife, guarding her after a long party to celebrate my second divorce. She never goes home. A new car appears in the driveway, a washer and dryer, paint on all the walls, a couch and chairs, new terrain for the rodents. We argue about buying clothes and power tools, endless repairs, abandoning the house and moving west. Late at night, the owls taunt me with questions but the scratching never stops. My wife claims I am the only one who hears the noise. She sleeps soundly under her new comforter while the sound in the walls rises to a crescendo.

Suddenly the scratching stops. I lie in bed trying to decipher the eerie silence like the moment after an earthquake when the wounded rock abruptly rests, or the moment after sex with a new partner, before the depression of closure and consequence sets in, a moment of exhaustion and dread. I feel down to the ends of my toes and fingers for grasping vines, but I sense nothing. Nor do I hear the growling of demon terriers or the whispered complaints of ex-wives.

Slowly I get up to check the house, tracing careful steps down the stairs and through the hushed forest. The night sky is clear, punctured by stars and still as death. I inhale the cold air. The wind begins slowly at first, refreshing in its briskness, but gradually it rises in strength, an icy breeze. A waft of artic air flings sharp edges of frozen snow from bare limbs of the maple trees, stinging my skin like needles. I close the door. Deep in the bowels of the cellar, the ancient furnace clicks and lights, beginning another cycle of warmth and chill, the beginning of my third divorce.

SHADOWS AND DREAMS

THE MAN WHO NEVER DREAMS

She hands me a cup of coffee,
steaming rich and sweet, one pass
through an unbleached filter,
her hands dry and cold from washing.
I see the damp towel hanging
on the back of a chair, unlike her,
always so tidy, and I realize the towel is mine,
my kitchen. She waits for an answer.

I study the rim and handle,
recalling the salt-glazed cup I received as a gift
stuffed with chocolates in bright foil wrappers,
and I feel a shock of sadness,
knowing my gift cup is broken, a cup she never knew.
She touches my arm, and her voice descends
from sadness to pity, flowing
sticky and sweet like honey into an empty cup.
The man who never dreams, she says.

I want to tell her how she misunderstood,
so I swing my legs up and around,
my feet landing flat on the floor

much too hard, the bed higher than I remember.
I smell the coffee, rich and thick,
steam beading on my head like sweat.
I look for my favorite cup, the chocolates
I have been saving for a moment like this,
and I shake my head as she spoons
honey into a stoneware cup.

I wish I could tell her something,
how I am dreaming now, dreaming of her,
how I prefer my coffee unsweetened,

but the steam wraps around me like a blanket.
One cup leads to another.

Her Collection of Knives

Evening wet and dark,
stars dimmed by humidity,
wine goblets sweating rings
on clear table top, revealing
its frame, cast iron with welded joints,
tiny hands supporting the glass,
still sea. No breeze, skin sticking.

She brings them out tray by tray,
sharp fingers, ground steel edges,
old ones tarnished, some gilded
daggers, sunk in leather sheaths,
arranged on black cloth
like cold, saintly ships.

Smile gleams in diffused light,
spaces between teeth, purple,
wine-soaked tongue. She perches
over the table, high cheek bones,
shoulders poised.

She locks the knives away,
their image lingering, glaze on steel,
damp breath on cold limbs. Her voice
lingers also, low soothing tones,
its stainless beauty.

Wine Stains

Our evening ends with stale champagne,
paper cups crushed,

reminding me of photographs
we brought back from London. Hands clasped
across the table, white cloth
absorbing our spilled wine.

I watch our images seep
into the fabric like the rings
of our cups: round, uneven, intersecting.

The next day, after your flight,
I reopen the bottle and trace each circle,
dipping my scissors
to edit our past and fill the empty spaces.

Stale bubbles rise and cling
to the grey wax of my cup,
bursting like words never spoken,
the letters we will never send.

They wait for us. Patches of linen
damp with age, a ring for every picture,
bubbles of breath, the bottle of wine
corked and saved.

HER NAMES

Names radiate from her like breath,
as if she gives life to every plant,
even Spanish moss in the highest
limbs of southern pine and azalea seedlings
along her front walk,
its slabs cracked and pitched
every which way like a pile
of brittle magnolia leaves.

In the sweat-stained afternoon,
we meet halfway up Oakdale Avenue,
her tall strides closing the gap between us
until we join, halves of the same seed,
while spring explodes around us:
tulip trees, dogwood, and cherry
blossoms burning red and pink,
petals clinging to her hair
as it flows and bounces in long
yellow clusters like wild forsythia.

In the evening we eat nothing
but flowers and drink Folonari wine,
always on sale in half-gallon bottles,
and we toast all things that escape
her naming, and she names them then,
some forgetting their names, as we
finally forget ours, drunk
with the thick perfume of May.

THE EMPTY BOTTLE

Clenching its neck,
you swing against the table's steel edge.
Stars burst around us,
shards of glass, blood-tinted wine
on skin.

Unable to move,
our clothes discarded for ritual,
the polished kitchen littered now
with edges, we stare
at the glass, ourselves.
We stare well into night,
air cold, stiff as wax.

I watch your hair turn grey,
canyons form on your face,
your flesh cooling under skin.
In a concave mirror
I see my own body
tighten with endless years.

If I could move now,
I would reach for the door.

Neither of us move.
We never break our pose,
never leave that room.

THE POISONED BLOOD

A survivor of lung cancer, Robert Moore
wants the doctors to test him,
a specimen to save others,
find the antibodies in his poisoned blood,
a polluted river too hot for tumors.

Find out how the grocery man,
stamper of cans, stacker of boxes,
green apron stained with purple ink,
suddenly became a poet.

How the former champion
high school wrestler lived
through surgery, months of treatment,
predictions of death, emerging
stronger, comparing himself
to death camp survivors. And why he
was banned by the Bridgeport coach
from wrestling the boys, the coach afraid
of injury, of poison. Find out why

the Value Food Stores stopped
his disability checks, why his wife
left the day he came home, why his children
and friends avoid him, although the poison
still causes him problems, too many to work.
No one can stand his success, he says,
how he runs at the high school track
and lives at the Market Street Hotel,
a Gulliver among the drunks and deserted,
his body a poem he yearns to tell.

The doctors ignore his letters.
When he tells me all of this
in the first minutes we meet, I watch
the shadows of the others departing
and look for an exit.

Light and Shadow

She says the light bothers her.
The fluorescent bulbs flicker,
so I change them.

But the artificial light
resonates and causes waves,
so I move her to a window

where sunlight burns
through morning fog. But the sun
is too bright for her, so I filter it
with blinds and shades, its ideal angle
tilted by her medication.

Then her room seems dim to me,
as if light were polarized
for one vanishing point,

like the leaning structures
of Van Gogh's farm: his colors
blended by brush and genius,
by madness.

Strokes of cloud, waves, and sky,
the light ripples around the burning
source, its spectrum absorbing all.

But she can only squint
with the glare she cannot describe.
I know her pain by its shadows.
To her I am the shadow.

LAST WORDS

The highway bends like metal
heated and warped,
the spring of a clock twisting
stem and movement,
gear teeth and ratchet.

Seconds click
like a surveyor's transit,
elevations obscured
by gravel and dust.

Words cure in pavement,
stains of rubber and exhaust,
cheeks aching from wind
and sand, lips pressing
the wall of air.

Then silence,
thick with humidity, our lives,
the sense of something lost,
foil ribbon unwinding,
gift unwrapped, empty.

TWO WOMEN LEAVING THE CHURCH

You wait until the sleet stops. Maple wings
spin down from trees. Dogs bark
when you start your mother's car,

the pock-marked Chevy, curb feelers
swaying with potholes, lipstick tissues
in a plastic bag. You carry
her purse. It's always the same,

she said, they help you out the door,
hand you refrigerated flowers, rub
their callouses on your cheek. Back home,
you smooth her photo, taping it

to the mirror you shared. You add the date
to your Bible, stuffed to its spine
with scentless roses, all the verses
she marked.

POEM WITH NUDE

Magazines in the attic, carefully preserved,
remind me of trips to the museum
where teachers hurried us past nudes
on the wall, nudes on pedestals, nudes on postcards,
nudes. In the attic I became a patron,
learning what artists have always known,
that few will pause before a painting of Venus
in a habit or a statue of David in full armor.

When I first entered Mona Lisa's room
at the Louvre, I learned something else. Her eyes
stared and followed me, undressing me as I approached.
Now I add a mysterious woman to this poem:
pensive, graceful, conversant in art and literature,
a poetry lover. Her expectant eyes undress you
as you read these lines. You might prefer
a robust, sensual man, a poet. I am tall,
with Olympic contours of flesh
and thick hair the hue of Aegean cliffs, my eyes
shine with the optimism of youth. Imagine
David on the beach at Corfu, your ideal,
your art.

At the Leonard Cohen Concert

Man in a black fedora reads Kant
sitting on a couch outside the men's room
in the historic Fox Theater in Oakland.
Wallpaper with Greek columns and heroes,
gold and bronze paint, a fluted pedestal
with branches reaching upward like worshippers
from a glazed vase. Couch with red
and black stripes on cream satin
knit with tiny stars, a tribute to performers,
their perceptions of space and time. Faint echoes
of former shows and films, clicks
of cells pulled through a hot projector,
faces dotted with lint, shades of gray
and Technicolor. The author's name
on the cover, black letters hovering
over his bust. Thoughts weave
with the voice of the singer
introducing a new song, muffled
by distant speakers and thick carpets.
Backup singers with perfect pitch
stand around his centered posture,
cocked knee over woolen thigh. The brim

of his fedora leans with his forehead,
projecting pure reason, his argument
for himself.

COMFORT FOOD

Image of Jesus appears on a Franco-American spaghetti billboard along the Martha Berry Highway. I drive past, missing him. She shows me the Atlanta Journal photograph, tracing his aquiline nose and thick hair flowing down from the open can, red-gold label and orange sauce adorning white strands, a pallet for comforting eyes and full lips saying so much without speaking a word. Pilgrims visit the site, building a shrine to the miracle with bouquets and wooden crosses. Soon workers return and paste up a new ad for Borden Milk, rolling over his image. She blames demons for the desecration and my disbelief, counting hundreds of spaghetti billboards posted on highways, but only this one shone with his image. She prays for me. I ask too many questions. I know we count by nature, counting even demons, as I count prescription tablets before my next refill, tablespoons of coffee beans left in a pound, laps I run in a race, when to sprint before the finish, breaths I have left. I know each can of spaghetti from reading the label. Same ingredients: corn syrup, sodium, calories. The flowing strands of pasta and sauce look so tempting, but I never eat canned spaghetti because it reminds me of all I am missing.

WATER'S EDGE

WEATHER REPORT

You wrote these letters at your cherry desk,
snow falling like cryptograms
outside your window, there in the deepest plains
where twisting winds suspend flakes
like lost mail. And I wait

on an unnamed hill in New York state
on the farthest ridge from the Catskills,
where sounds diminish with old age
like the hills themselves, waiting
for signs of snow, fronts moving east.

We never wrote letters before,
never needed the cold precision of writing,
sharing an immunity to weather
that language could never distort.
Now I defy the weather,

diving in the deepest drift, sinking
with my heat, skin soaked with your words.
In spring they will break me out,
ship me home to Nebraska,

still alive, breathing slowly
like a dormant bear, a thicker, warmer
letter than you expected.

LIFE LINE

One line in my palm is the life line,
that much I know. When I squeeze my hand,
the stretched skin and calluses fold unevenly
like creases in an old snapshot.

A line of people wait outside Ideal Coffee
staring at screens, headphones fixed,
wrapping around the corner like knotted rope
stretched between poles and connected
from phone to phone the way electricity traces
a magnetic field around the curve
of earth. Charged ions pull north and south
like cars at rush hour, each with its own destination
seeming random but fixed in a pattern. Waves
from the San Lorenzo River push waves
from the ocean while the surf washes over sand,
drops pebbles and shells like lost messages,
and carves new lines in the beach. The edge
recedes year by year, cliff road sliding,
steps of asphalt where cars once drove.

In the restaurant hangs a photograph,
black and white, muscle cars waiting in three lines
on Beach Street. Young people lean out
their windows, hair sculpted in perfect arcs,
surfboards on their roofs all pointing
the same direction. I shut my eyes and see
the film negative, sky dark in afternoon sunlight,
where cars flow out like kelp on an ebbing tide
and kids smile with black teeth and pale faces,
their life lines gray on darker hands like weathered planks
between tar-stained pilings of the wharf.

I would join them, reverse my quantum spin,
let it pull me back through my headphones,
follow ions where they lead, back to the flash.
Then I might squeeze my hand and stretch
my weathered skin tighter, more subtle,
pale and soft like a child's.

SNOW SQUALL

Highway wet, black
as cancer when it hits,
blinding in headlights,
white streaks twist
like maggots. I brake,
my eyes parched
by the snow's fever,
drive on, knowing
clusters will stick,
seal off my sight,
my air. Snow fills up
ditches, obscures lines,
white pulp bursting. Snow
clings to my wipers
and presses against my motion
like sleep. I remember
her heavy white blankets,
flannel sheets damp
with sweat, pulse
slowing. Then it stops.
At the crest of a hill
the squall breaks,

torn by rain.
Night pours in,
warm, liquid night.

CIDER PRESS

Like apples dropped in a pile,
our skin grows softer and falls,
outlines fading
in the mattress of earth.

One day you decide to get up,
but I talk you down,
hesitations smothered
like grass beneath our soggy flesh.

When sunlight breaks in,
we embrace the same illusion,
our bodies turning
our fermented breath.

ICE AGE

Spreading cold hands,
the glacier splits and extends.
Each finger presses a valley, each nail
carves a lake. The wall of ice
pushes southward year by year.
We sense it now, our summers gray,
breathing deeply to hold our air,
old friends leaving us behind.

We accept our roles as scientists,
record each colder day, every inch
of snow proving our predictions.

In the shortened spring we walk
as we always did, but quicker now
to warm our blood, hats pulled down
on thinning hair. In the night,
we hear blades of ice scraping
mounds of snow like huge trucks,
smashing pavement as they come.
The air cracks our breath,
ice blocks our doors.

THE MUSEUM OF PERSONAL HISTORY

You clutch your memories like relics of saints
and snarl at me when I come too close.
You know I intend to violate them.

I walk softly like an outlaw,
searching your attic and empty sheds,
turning through the compost behind the barn.

I see your history form itself
as a silhouette defined by clues I discover
and the things you never say.

I correct the figure with locks of hair,
chips of wood, pieces of cloth—
new exhibits for your collection.

Like a child who makes an angel in snow,
waving his arms to carve giant wings,
I imprint a fossil of myself.

READING THE SIGNS

Turning my cards face up she says,
You are the shore to my ocean.
Her chart of constellations
fixed with names of gods and heroes
forgotten except for moments like this.
My signs are all earth signs.

In the night sky the ancient lines
stretch with time, strain for meaning.
Northern lights break in waves,
tides dragging heartbeats of current,
shoreline cliff crumbling,
sand between fingers.

Candles flicker on table top.
Fluorescent lights mimic stars,
tenuous spectrums pulling
my focus closer, eyes squeezing shut,
trying to read a new pattern.

The Empress of Iowa Sheds Her Disguise

She tells me what to expect,
and I imagine the rest:
a girl alone in the cornfield,

the stalks a tall fence.
Her corn silk hair darkens with age
like clouds in an August

sky. She sees thunderheads form
and ducks her head for cover.
Later, unfolding like a leaf,

she reaches toward the sun
as if the sun were her lover
or reminded her of what a lover

might be. But when she turns
to me, I know what to do,
as any farmer would. I switch

on the lamp and offer her water,
leaching her roots until they are soft,
and return her to her soil.

Turning Back at the Rubicon

We had thought of sending you to the desert
to satisfy your yearning for a frontier
where you would have to bring water.

There you would reach deep into sand
and reap a harvest of echoes
between bleached rock and sky.

And you would become the focus of these echoes
and the weariness of empire,
stalking desert like Santa Ana wind.

But here you will have a home.
We have cultivated a garden for you
with mounds of hybrid vines.

One day you will remember this moment
but only as a dryness of breath
as you wind among rows,
questioning the melons.

The Rattlesnake Exchanges Its Skin

Rattlesnake searches for heat,
crawls into your sleeping bag, you feel
its cold mass press against flesh.

You unzip slowly,
not to disturb, hoping
it will seek the morning sun.

Sometimes you wake up alone
and find flakes of molted skin.

Other mornings you discover
strands of hair, cotton threads,
the sour scent of sleep,

signs that you have stalked
the blanket den and coiled there,

absorbing heat, striking unrestrained
at her sudden fear,
miles from any town.

Smelling the Rain

Water flowed through bark canyons,
elm and planks of weathered pine,
our fort in the farmyard.

That day my foot slipped,
falling down on muddy shards
of slate and cow bones,
my knee scraped and bleeding,
arm twisted like a thin stalk
straining to lift a heavy bloom
of dandelion sun.

You were there,
wrist slung in tee shirt,
fingernails caked with mud,
wrapping my wounds in grass,
your green shoots growing up
through holes in my shoes.

Now my blue jeans drag,
worn cuffs soaked in puddles,
but you are still there

in your forever spring,
waiting so we can climb again
one more time on bending limb.

Door of Echoes

THE BOXER'S CHOICE

My grandfather ran without a platform,
independent, a referee. Like Jack Dempsey
in his New York restaurant, he recalled every face,
even those he never met,
with a faith he would know them
when he spoke their will in the House
and a faith they would know him
for the good man he was. A salesman,
he sold for little profit, always discounts
for churches and youth groups. He won
good will in the Catholic neighborhoods
but too few votes in the Primary.

That summer, politicians and old boxers
called at his house. I liked the boxers best,
their stretched tee-shirts, knotted muscles.
They worked stiff-legged jobs and spoke
in whispers to hide their accents
when they showed me trophies won
at the settlement house and given
to their Irish coach who liked
helping boys better than selling

office machines. They brought him corned beef,
root beer, and stories. The food more generous
and stories longer as years passed.
The politicians drank their whiskey
and left, but the boxers stayed on,
a wink and a shuffle most nights
until the old man died.

Grandfather Fishing

Tackle clean and orderly,
lures stored in sales boxes,
red and yellow doll flies for crappie,
bass spoons, glittering minnows,
green and gold La-Z-Ikes
for muskie and pickerel.

Seldom catches a fish, testing
his newest lure, solving
the mystery of water and hunger,
leaning over the lake, the way he fixes cars
by listening, pipe smoldering,
pointing his stem at the failing part,
carburetor, points, valves, or worse.

One day his heart stops.
He pounds his chest with his fists
and drives himself to the hospital
where he floats on calm water,
guiding its repair.

MY ONLY HOME RUN

Eight years old,
the baseball my grandfather saved
from a burnt-out store, fire
imprinted in rawhide, brown stain
lost in scuffs, but never its scent
of smoked hotdogs, re-stitched
with nylon thread until the cover wore off,
wrapped in black electrical tape,
shining like any playground ball.

But when I rub it with spit
and squeeze my glove,
pocket pressed to my face
like an oxygen cup,
I smell the lingering fire,
ball flashing over cottonwoods,
ascending out of view.

Shaky Charlie Talks About His Youth

In North Dakota, we plant early
and open ditches before the river thaws.
The water you get must last.
We sow more seed each year than we'll need,
in case the spring's dry and the summer's hot,
or the cattle will die next winter.

He said this at harvest time on the Marne,
in the earthquake evenings with no stars,
the farmland shaking like a slaughtered cow,
and in the machine gun mornings, the tin cups,
the coffee burning his numb lips.

He said it again, alone in the muddy trench,
his hearing stunned, his limbs quaking.
He was saying it when they found him,
and he repeated it like a liturgy
to sterile hospital walls.

Forty years later, he still talks about it
as his sister smiles and helps him drink
coffee. Her grandchildren laugh at his stories—

Shaky Charlie. Every month she drives him to Fargo
where he says it again and the doctor laughs.
They all remember the prairie of his youth.

What to Do in Case of a Gas Attack

My father dug a trench for his fear.
By the time he returned,
his blisters had healed and no Axis planes
had bombed Minnesota.
With his uncashed checks, he bought a mortgage,
a two-story house, brick, no cellar,
an attic with no windows.

Upstairs, he built a shower
and a locker for dry goods:
beans, canned peaches, condensed milk, and flour.
A baking soda solution, bleaching solution,
and soap.

Sometimes I heard him climb
the stairs at night
to check his provisions.
Some nights he heard the sirens
and clutched my mother's arm.
Some nights he never stopped climbing,
up through the roof,
above the heavy clouds.

My Father's Tools

Leaning over typewriter frame, hands
ink dark with calluses, my father reaches
around type bars and brackets, levers
of tempered steel, hooking a spring,
placing the smallest screw
with magnetized driver. He adjusts
to touch, aligning letters
until they flow in perfect lines,
finger strike to paper.

Broken machines wait on bench
with glass jars of spare parts,
needle-nosed pliers worn smooth,
small torch for soldering type,
hooks, benders, crimpers,
oil can with long nozzle,
cleaning tub with black solvent.

He lets me scrub the type
and pivots, bathe them in oil,
wipe them dry until they shine
like reborn souls. Now the typewriters

are gone but I keep his tools,
fixing any problem. I show my son
how to grasp each one, correct angle,
knowing the tool by its function.
He adds his layer of fingerprints,
imagining machines he will build.

LEARNING HOW TO DREAM

I stare at my hands
like Don Juan in the desert,
turning my palms upward
to catch my dream,
a splash of rain
no instrument can trace.

The lines inscribe a language
stamped by age, folded tendons,
shards of skin etched like sediment.

My younger hand, once unmarked,
pressed into my mother's,
dry to my touch, her scent of water
evaporating like morning fog
seeping through the desert floor,
a hidden reservoir.

She holds my father's hand
pitted with machine oil,
swinging me between them.

When I awaken,
I study my hands
to recover the trail.
I squeeze my mother's hand,
feeling it smaller, fragile
like my son's hand
reaching for my thumb
to pull himself up.

WHEN IT WAS DARK ENOUGH

My father seldom talked about the war,
as if nothing had happened, but he talked
in his sleep. My mother never understood
what he said. Some attacks were malaria
and she fetched his quinine tablets.

He sat up sweating, clutching her arm,
nightmare unspoken. Water in her hands
cooled his sudden temper even in daylight.
When he first came home, his darkness
scared his mother. He wanted to start
a new religion, all false.

He brought back few souvenirs. Wooden shoes
for his sisters and an Arab knife—a gift
from North Africa, handle sun-bleached wood
wrapped with coat hanger wire, steel blade
sharpened by hand and bent in waves
from opening K-ration cans. He gave away

the chocolate bars and most cigarettes.
He told us he picked bugs out of his mess kit
until he decided they tasted pretty good.
Then he caught more and dropped them in.
We knew the war by his jokes. He was the only son;
his sisters all married veterans. They sat in a circle

at our family picnics, hands wrapped around necks
of brown beer bottles, red coals of cigarettes
rising in gesture and sinking to mouth and armrest,
quietly talking over the drone of mosquitoes
after their wives sought the safety of the porch.

We crept closer to hear what they said,
but they pulled their silence tighter around them
like an oily tarp on night watch, darkness descending
until they finally said it was dark enough
to light the firecrackers they brought.
They held their ears and smiled.

FAMILY DINNER

Table seldom used for dinners,
a place to rest bags and boxes
from car to bedroom, cellar,
storage, books we might read,
photographs we should hang.

Family shifts on stiff chairs,
cushions covered in plastic,
hot in summer air, while I joke,
recalling dinners with my parents.
Father at head of table
filling the shortest silence,
all of us attentive, lest he notice,
mother apologizing, the later times
she fixed my favorite meal
hoping I might show up.

Children cross long legs,
remembering words
I still avoid, boxes

from my parents' house
piled in the attic,
never opened.

BLUEGILL

Dead in the field,
fish eyes stare at noon sun
through clouded lenses. Four bluegills
scattered around a rough wicker creel,
yellow reeds matching the dried grass,
goldenrod, thistle and milkweed stems
with tufts of seeds hanging like lint.
Blood trails along one gill, one tail curls
in mid flip. My friend whispers, *Indians,*
hardly audible above traffic.
Maybe they will return.

But we know the truth, searching for signs,
broken stalks from moccasin steps
or pony hooves. Ojibwe leave no trails,
pass in the silence of night, crossing our dreams
from one turtle island of refuge to another:
Montreal, Niagara Falls,
Detroit harbor, across Lake Superior
to the St. Louis River, Great Plains,

ever westward. We haunt their spirit dreams,
push them ahead like a cool breeze
announcing a storm, weather they try to escape.

They know our people by the land,
the changes they see, bluegills thrown
from the window of a passing car
left to rot on roadside weeds.

THE CROSSING

At the crossing we count box cars,
the bumper of our '57 Chevy waits.
We look past the seat stains, the only time
our dad bought Dairy Queen, and watch
for bums sleeping on wheel frames
or standing in doorways. We wave
despite my mother's glare, they wave back.
She says bums will steal us but I know better.

They live in the freight yard
deep in Minneapolis where one afternoon I yelled
and a bum chased my friends and me.
We climbed a linked steel fence
and leapt to the other side. He grabbed the wire,
reaching through the square holes,
his arms thin as rusted tail pipe, brown
and wrinkled, too weak to climb,
rough skin covering his body,
his face. His few teeth and parched lips
cursed us back, sounding hollow and dry.

None of us spoke, feeling guilty,
knowing the safety of the fence was more than that,
a barrier between worlds, only touching
in secret places like this. He smiled at me,
his gesture more frightening than his pursuit,
as if he knew me well. We ran for our bikes
and silently pedaled home. I never told anyone

what really happened, how thin arms now
hang from my shirtsleeves,
how I am dead to some, hardly alive to others.
I count cars behind lowered barriers,
watch the children's clear faces, hands waving
over parents' shoulders, and I wish
one more Dairy Queen for each of them.

ACKNOWLEDGMENTS

The author would like to thank the following literary journals in which these poems first appeared.

Abraxas: "The Poisoned Blood"

Blue Buildings: "Two Women Leaving the Church"

California Quarterly: "The Rattlesnake Exchanges Its Skin"

Centennial Review: "The Museum of Personal History"

Chattahoochee Review: "The Empress of Iowa Sheds Her Disguise" and "Cider Press"

Cold Creek Review: "Light and Shadow"

Contact II: "Widow's Peak"

Concerning Poetry: "Turning Back at the Rubicon" and "How to Build a House"

Cottonwood Review: "Shaky Charlie Talks About His Youth"

formercactus: "My Only Homerun"

Front Porch Review: "Family Dinner"

Great River Review: "Poem With Nude" and "My Old Furnace"

Green Light Literary Journal: "Life Line"

Kalliope: "Painting the House White"

Kansas Quarterly: "The Boxer's Choice"

The Lake: "Bluejay"

Literally Stories: "My Third Divorce"

Lullwater Review: "Her White Tattoo"

The Mantle: "Smelling the Rain"

Milkweed Chronicle: "Weather Report" and "The Weeping Willows Green First"

Poetry at 33: "Wine Stains"

Poetry Motel: "The Man Who Never Dreams"

Poetry Northwest: "The Poet's Garage"

Poetry Quarterly: "Last Words"

Puerto del Sol: "The Empty Bottle"

Rat's Ass Review: "At the Leonard Cohen Concert"

Riggwelter: "Ice Age"

South Dakota Review: "The Lives of a Cell" and "What to Do in the Case of a Gas Attack"

Split Rock Review: "The Crossing"

Third Wednesday: "Her Names"

Trinity Review: "Bluegill"

Valparaiso Poetry Review: "When It Was Dark Enough"

Westward Quarterly: "What the Seagulls Know"

ABOUT TERRY TIERNEY

Terry writes poetry and fiction. He was born in South Dakota and raised in Minneapolis and Cleveland, where his parents moved when he was in high school. After serving in the Seabees, he received a BA and MA in English from SUNY Binghamton, and a PhD in Victorian Literature from Emory University. He taught college students for a few years before moving into software engineering where he survived several Silicon Valley startups. He lives in the San Francisco Bay Area with his wife and son. Please visit his website at http://terrytierney.com.

ABOUT THE PRESS

Unsolicited Press is a small press in Portland, Oregon. The publisher produces exemplary fiction, poetry, and creative nonfiction.

Learn more at unsolicitedpress.com.

CPSIA information can be obtained
at www.ICGtesting.com
Printed in the USA
FSHW010727170220

9 781950 730414